HARRIET TUBMAN

ABOLITIONIST AND CONDUCTOR OF THE UNDERGROUND RAILROAD

WOMEN WHO CHANGED HISTORY

HARRIET TUBMAN

ABOLITIONIST AND CONDUCTOR OF THE UNDERGROUND RAILROAD

BARBARA KRASNER

Britannica Educational Publishing

IN ASSOCIATION WITH

ROSEN

EDUCATIONAL SERVICES

Published in 2018 by Britannica Educational Publishing (a trademark of Encyclopædia Britannica, Inc.) in association with The Rosen Publishing Group, Inc.
29 East 21st Street, New York, NY 10010

Distributed exclusively by Rosen Publishing.
To see additional Britannica Educational Publishing titles, go to rosenpublishing.com.

First Edition

Britannica Educational Publishing
J.E. Luebering: Executive Director, Core Editorial
Andrea R. Field: Managing Editor, Compton's by Britannica

Rosen Publishing
Heather Moore Niver: Editor
Nelson Sá: Art Director
Michael Moy: Designer
Cindy Reiman: Photography Manager
Heather Moore Niver: Photo Researcher

Library of Congress Cataloging-in-Publication Data

Names: Krasner, Barbara, author.
Title: Harriet Tubman : abolitionist and conductor of the underground railroad / Barbara Krasner.
Description: First edition. | New York, NY : Britannica Educational Publishing, 2018. | Series: Women who changed history | Includes bibliographical references and index.
Identifiers: LCCN 2016057945| ISBN 9781680486599 (library bound : alk. paper)| ISBN 9781680486575 (pbk. : alk. paper) | ISBN 9781680486582 (6-pack : alk. paper)
Subjects: LCSH: Tubman, Harriet, 1820?-1913—Juvenile literature. | Slaves—United States—Biography—Juvenile literature. | African American women—Biography—Juvenile literature. | Underground Railroad—Juvenile literature.
Classification: LCC E444.T82 K73 2017 | DDC 973.71/15092 [B] —dc23
LC record available at https://lccn.loc.gov/2016057945

Manufactured in the United States of America

Photo credits: Cover Universal History Archive/Universal Images Group/Getty Images; p. 7 Underwood Archives/Archive Photos/Getty Images; p. 10 Artepics/Alamy Stock Photo; p. 11 Kean Collection/Archive Photos/Getty Images; pp. 12–13 Everett Historical/Shutterstock.com; pp. 14, 32–33 Bettman/Getty Images; p. 17 Chicago History Museum/Archive Photos/Getty Images; p. 18 Private Collection/Wood Ronsaville Harlin, Inc./Bridgeman Images; p. 19 Hulton Archive/Archive Photos/Getty Images; p. 21 Library of Congress/Corbis Historical/Getty Images; p. 22 National Geographic Creative/Alamy Stock Photo; p. 25 Afro Newspaper/Gado/Archive Photos/Getty Images; pp. 27, 36, 39 Photos.com/Thinkstock; p. 28 debra millet/Shutterstock.com; p. 31 GL Archive/Alamy Stock Photo; p. 34 Andrew Lichtenstein/Corbis Historical/Getty Images; p. 40 Buyenlarge/Archive Photos/Getty Images; p. 41 stockelements/Shutterstock.com; p. 43 Hulton Archive/Getty Images.

CONTENTS

INTRODUCTION

Harriet Tubman was born Araminta Ross around 1820 on a plantation near Bucktown, Maryland, on the eastern shores of Chesapeake Bay. Her parents, Harriet Green and Benjamin Ross, were slaves. That meant Araminta would be a slave, too. She had ten siblings. Above all else, Araminta wanted her large family to stick together. Two of her sisters had already been sold, carried off farther south despite their protests and tears. Her mother stood before her as a powerful example of resistance. She had hidden one of Araminta's brothers for a month with friends in the woods from a Georgia slave buyer. From her mother she learned just how strong a woman could be.

As early as age five, Araminta was hired out to help care for a white baby. At such a young age, she was not at all prepared for the responsibility. Her mistress whipped her five times every morning to make sure she did her work. Sixty years later, she still bore the scars around her neck to prove it. She continued to be hired out to do housework and care for white children on nearby farms. Quick-thinking and clever, Araminta soon adopted habits that cleverly protected her against her mistress' whippings. She would wear as much clothing as possible and when about to receive the usual morning punishments she would cry out as if she had felt the full force of the whip.

By the age of twelve, she made the transition from an inside slave to a farmhand helping with the harvest. But

Born a slave, Harriet Tubman risked her life to bring others to safety and to serve her country as a Union spy.

she could no longer defend herself from beatings. When an overseer tried to harm a field worker for deserting his post, Araminta blocked the overseer's path—her first act of defiance. His temper raging, he struck her on the head with a piece of iron. Despite the head covering she wore, the wounds ran deep, breaking her skull. She was carried back to her owner with the message that she was no longer worth anything. Her family worried she would not recover from the injury. Her owner tried to sell her, but no one offered to buy. Her family's prayers were eventually answered. Although it took months, she healed. However, as a result of the blow, she would fall asleep suddenly several times a day for the rest of her life.

Despite the injury, Araminta grew strong. She hauled flour barrels onto carts. She was hired out with her father and brothers to cut and haul timber. Soon she was chopping more wood than most men. She exceeded what was expected of her. She gained physical stamina. She grew accustomed to back-breaking work. At the same time, she relied on her faith to get her through the day. She would need that strength of body and mind to realize her own destiny. Araminta's father's owner died in 1836 and Ben Ross was granted his freedom several years later. He stayed on the plantation, though, working as a timber inspector. Araminta wanted more. She wanted to run free. She wanted her whole family to run free. She wanted all slaves to run free.

CHAPTER ONE

VISIONS NORTH

Araminta Ross married John Tubman, a free black man, in 1844. She took her husband's surname, and around that time she also changed her first name to Harriet, after her beloved mother. The laws at that time outlawed any marriage between a slave and a free black. Instead, it was considered an informal arrangement. The slave's owner could completely ignore it. That also meant that the slave and any of the slave's children could be sold at whim, since a child born to a slave was automatically put into bondage. However, after her father gained his freedom in 1840, Tubman wanted to explore her own status. She believed that her mother may have mistakenly been kept a slave after her first owner died. In 1845 she hired a lawyer and he investigated the matter. The lawyer and other white authorities determined that her mother, Harriet Ross, could have been freed when she turned forty-five. But because Tubman's mother had been passed as property from owner to owner, it was unclear whether she could still be freed. Tubman nevertheless vowed to free herself. To do so would involve a long, dangerous journey to the North.

Tubman's heroic acts have been memorialized through art, including this twentieth-century painting by African American artist William H. Johnson. He emphasizes the North Star as her guiding force.

FREE BLACKS AND SLAVES

Even before President Abraham Lincoln issued the Emancipation Proclamation in 1863, which freed the slaves of the Confederate states in rebellion against the Union, not all blacks in America were born into or stayed in slavery. Some blacks gained their freedom after his or her owner died, through the owner's will. Others were freed at a certain age, like Tubman's father, Ben Ross. Still others escaped to the North for their freedom. There were also immigrants from the West Indies who arrived in America on their own who were never slaves. The American Revolution sparked a movement to free slaves to serve in the militia. The Louisiana Purchase of 1803 brought with it thousands of free blacks, whose existence came as the result of relationships between French and Spanish colonists and slaves. There were more free blacks living in the South than there ever were living in the North.

President Lincoln's decree to free the slaves became the Emancipation Proclamation. Note the bolded words: "All persons held as slaves…shall be free."

POWERFUL DREAMS, GUIDING VISIONS

Tubman had visions, or dreams she thought were sending her clear messages of freedom. They came to her while she was fully awake. One vision in particular depicted men on horseback galloping to round up slaves. Ear-piercing shrieks and the clapping of horse hooves filled her ears. It was an unforgettable nightmare. But she also had vivid visions of flying across fields and mountains, seeing women in white who would pull her across the landscape.

OFF AND RUNNING

By 1849, Tubman feared being sold farther south. She had heard her brothers might be sold, too. She prayed her owner would be more Christian and set them free. When she saw no evidence of that, she prayed for his death. She believed he had no legal right to keep her and her family in slavery. Her prayers seemed to be answered when her owner suddenly died that year. But her owner's death put her at a crossroads. She asked herself many questions about how her mother and brothers and sisters would get along. Would the entire family now be split up? Would she be sold and separated from her husband?

Tubman knew she had to take an active role in her own destiny. She was entitled to liberty or death, and

Tubman's arrival in Philadelphia could have resembled the scene below, with refugee slaves scrambling to safety from the banks of the Schuylkill River with the help of friends.

SPEAKING OUT AGAINST SLAVERY

Kidnapped Africans were brought to America as slaves as early as 1619. Even people in the North owned slaves. But by the 1820s, many in the North began to feel that no man should own another. One man, William Lloyd Garrison, started a newspaper called the *Liberator*. It came out clearly against slavery, and Garrison became a well-known and outspoken abolitionist. Groups of people banded together and risked their lives to help runaway slaves reach freedom. Members of certain religious groups, such as Quakers, Methodists, and Mennonites, did not believe in slavery and offered help. A Quaker group near the area from which Tubman had escaped gave shelter and guidance. A secret network formed. It was called the Underground Railroad. Pennsylvania saw particularly heavy traffic along this network.

LADIES' DEPARTMENT.

'Am I not a Woman and a Sister?'

White Lady, happy, proud and free,
Lend awhile thine ear to me;
Let the Negro Mother's wail
Turn thy pale cheek still more pale.
Can the Negro Mother joy
Over this her captive boy,
Which in bondage and in tears,
For a life of wo she rears?
Though she bears a Mother's name,
A Mother's rights she may not claim;
For the white man's will can part,
Her darling from her bursting heart.

From the Genius of Universal Emancipation.

LETTERS ON SLAVERY.—No. III.

Garrison's paper, the *Liberator,* carried this antislavery poem calling out to white women in the name of solidarity of all women and mothers, regardless of color.

she would take whichever one came to her. She left her husband in the fall of 1849 and traveled at night on foot. Most fugitives were men, but Tubman had the strength of a man. Her owner's widow posted an advertisement offering a $100 reward for her return. As she made her way through Delaware into Pennsylvania, she received help from the Underground Railroad. Tubman was so grateful for the assistance, she gave one helpful woman a treasured homemade quilt. Finally, she arrived safely in Philadelphia and started a new life in freedom. She later described the moment when she finally crossed into free territory: "When I found I had crossed that line, I looked at my hands to see if I was the same person. There was such a glory over everything; the sun came like gold through the trees, and over the fields, and I felt like I was in Heaven."

CHAPTER TWO

LET MY PEOPLE GO

Historians still debate the actual origin of the Underground Railroad. One account refers to a story about a Kentucky slave in 1831. He escaped his master and the master believed he had taken an underground road. Another account appeared in 1839 when a Washington, DC, reporter wrote in a local newspaper about a tortured slave who revealed he was supposed to go north on an underground railroad to Boston, Massachusetts. But some believe the Underground Railroad began as early as 1810. This secret network was formed by individuals who were unhappy with the Fugitive Slave Act of 1793.

Whatever the origin, the Underground Railroad was real, although it was neither underground nor a railroad. The Underground Railroad adopted railway terms. Slaves were called "freight" or "cargo." Routes were called "lines." A stopping place was a "station." And people who helped the runaways along the Underground Railroad were called "conductors."

An organized escape system that operated by word of mouth, the railroad helped slaves from the South escape

This 1844 Chicago advertisement for the Liberty Line actually refers to the Underground Railroad. It promises free seats irrespective of color for passengers seeking a northern route to Canada.

to the Northern states and Canada. The network of routes extended in all directions throughout fourteen Northern states from Maine to Nebraska and helped between 40,000 to 100,000 slaves (out of 3.5 million slaves) reach freedom. The exact number is difficult to pinpoint, because the railroad operated in extreme secrecy; it kept few records. Although only a small group of Northerners participated, the railroad stirred Northern sympathy for the slaves. This convinced many Southerners that the North would not allow slavery to continue for much longer.

When Harriet "Moses" Tubman appeared at a slave's door, there was no time to waste. The time to run was now.

ANSWERING THE CALL TO DUTY

Although Philadelphia, Pennsylvania, boasted a large community of free blacks, Tubman could not stop thinking of all those left behind in the South. She knew she had to go back and bring as many people as she could to safety. She appeared mysteriously out of the night at slave cabins on plantations where anxious freedom-seekers awaited her. They waited for "Moses," Tubman's code name.

Tubman worked closely with the Underground Railroad. All the wages she had earned when she was working as a maid in hotels and clubs in Philadelphia were poured into her rescue operations. Tubman knew the risks involved. She had to exercise strict discipline. If anyone in her care decided to take a rest or drop out and return to slavery, she pulled out her revolver. She forced them to pull their weary bodies from the ground and continue the long, treacherous journey.

Shown with a rifle in this circa 1865 portrait, Tubman meant business. On their dangerous trek north, fleeing slaves had to obey her rules.

THE FUGITIVE SLAVE ACTS

The first American law involving slavery was passed in 1793. It was called the Fugitive Slave Act. This law made it a crime to give refuge to an escaped slave or to interfere with his or her arrest. It allowed capture and return even if the slave escaped to another state or US territory. In 1850, a new, stricter law was passed as part of a set of compromises made with the South. The law now penalized federal marshals who refused to enforce the law and individuals who helped slaves escape. If caught, fugitives would not be able to testify in court on their own behalf. They also would not be permitted a jury trial. This law was so severe that it intensified the abolitionist movement. The acts were finally repealed in 1864 near the end of the Civil War.

GO DOWN, MOSES

Slave catchers were always close behind. Now faced with the consequences of the Fugitive Slave Act of 1850, Tubman and her followers were in greater peril than ever. She had to reroute her efforts from New York, her usual destination, to Canada. She had to take extra measures to keep everyone in her care safe. By 1856, there was a $40,000 reward for her capture. By comparison, an average worker around that time earned only about $300 a

Refugees on the run were prepared to make a "bold stroke for freedom" against slave catchers as shown in this engraving from William Still's 1872 book about the Underground Railroad.

year. Finding and capturing Tubman could make someone quite rich.

With danger at every turn, Tubman carefully planned her journeys. Although she could neither read nor write, she was brilliant at considering options and alternatives.

In this painting, smiling faces and hands in prayer distinguish former slaves as Tubman delivers them to freedom in Canada. Tubman's revolver hangs at her waist.

She knew, too, she could only lead her people part of the way. She left fugitives in care of other Underground Railroad conductors. One of her signals to friendly forces that danger was in the area was singing, “Oh go down, Moses, way down into Egypt’s land, tell old Pharaoh, let my people go.”

She made nineteen dangerous journeys to the South over the course of eight years. Eventually she guided her parents and most of her brothers and sisters to the safety of the North. All told, she may have delivered three hundred people out of slavery. She said, “I never ran my train off the track, and I never lost a passenger.”

In Canada, American laws could not be enforced. Slave catchers had no authority there. The former slaves would be safe and free. Tubman herself settled in Ontario, Canada, for a while, until her next duty called her into action.

CHAPTER THREE

"GENERAL" TUBMAN

Even when not physically leading her people out of slavery, Tubman did not rest or give up her cause. She spoke at meetings and assemblies for abolitionists and women's rights supporters. To ensure slave hunters could not find her, she often concealed her name. For instance, at one talk in Boston in 1859, she used the name Harriet Garrison, fusing her name with that of the well-known abolitionist William Lloyd Garrison. She developed a network of friends who were known antislavery advocates. They were writers, publishers, speakers, and politicians, but most of all, they were people of action, just like Tubman. She became their fierce ally and lifelong friend.

As she looked forward to the day of emancipation for all slaves, she decided she needed to bring her family out of Canada. It was time to make a more direct attack on slavery.

This 1940 drawing shows Tubman as a powerful public speaker against slavery and for women's rights, a role she found necessary and satisfying.

WOMEN'S RIGHTS

By the mid-nineteenth century, a call for women's rights emerged in the United States. In 1848 a conference of women and men gathered in Seneca Falls, New York, to issue a declaration advocating for these rights. Led by antislavery leader Lucretia Mott and legal expert Elizabeth Cady Stanton, attendees debated and crafted a list of grievances concerning educational, vocational, economic, and religious inequality. Changes in the law would be necessary to balance the equality between women and men. This convention launched the women's rights movement that lasted into the twentieth century. After voting rights were finally granted to black males, abolitionist Susan B. Anthony of Rochester, New York, thought women ought to have that right, too. She helped to form the National Woman Suffrage Association. She, Stanton, and colleague Lucy Stone traveled the country to advocate for women's right to vote. Women gained this hard-earned right in 1920 through the Nineteenth Amendment to the US Constitution.

Many of these early fighters also opposed slavery. At the New York State Women's Suffrage Association in 1904, leader Susan B. Anthony introduced Tubman and held her hand. In freedom, Tubman became a passionate fighter for women's rights. Her efforts became legendary.

THE GENERAL AND JOHN BROWN

No one within Tubman's circle could have had more of a direct attack in mind than white abolitionist John Brown, whom Tubman met in 1858. He was a determined, even fanatical fighter against slavery. Brown believed slavery was

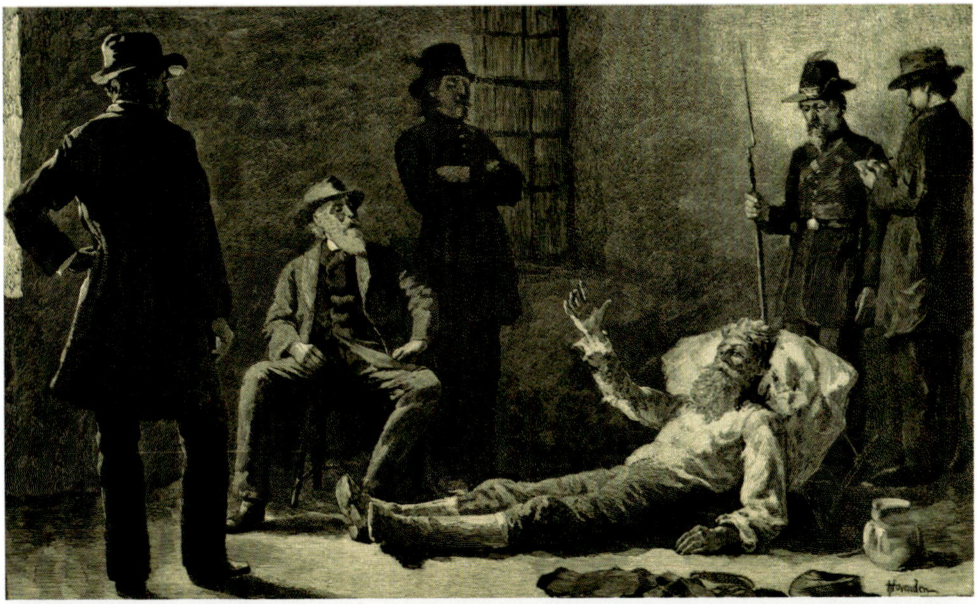

Abolitionist John Brown was captured and killed. His legend, however, remains. He was immortalized in the Union Army song "John Brown's Body."

a sin against Christianity. He also believed bloodshed was necessary to end slavery. In October 1859 Tubman assisted him in the planning for his attack on the federal armory in Harper's Ferry, Virginia (now in West Virginia). In admiration Brown dubbed her "General" Tubman. She promised Brown that many of the former slaves she had freed would join him. Only illness brought on by her old skull injury prevented her from fighting alongside Brown during the raid. Brown's meager army held out until his capture. Half his recruits, including two of his sons, were killed in the fight with the local militia. Brown was tried and found guilty of treason, murder, and inciting slaves to rebellion. He was hanged. But his actions brought him reverence and historians now believe his raid helped to hasten the Civil War.

A signpost in Auburn, New York, memorializes Tubman's home, calling her the "Moses of her people." Her home became a haven for refugee slaves.

STRUGGLES AT HOME IN AUBURN

In Auburn, New York, Tubman found a circle of antislavery advocates, too. The city served as a station for the Underground Railroad. Senator William Seward, long against slavery and later President Lincoln's secretary of state, lived there. When Tubman wanted a house of her own, he offered her one she could afford. She moved to Auburn in 1857. She brought her parents from Canada to live with her. She may have considered giving up her role as a conductor of the Underground Railroad and instead look for her new home to serve as a station and she the stationmaster. So many slaves still needed the help toward freedom.

Close to home, one of these was Charles Nalle, who had escaped to upstate New York from Virginia in 1858. The slavecatcher caught up with him in 1860 and now Nalle was being held by federal authorities in Troy. Tubman hatched a plan. She disguised herself as an elderly woman in order to gain access to Nalle and helped him flee from custody when he was brought out into the street where a large crowd had gathered. Despite receiving several blows to her head from officers, she ushered Nalle through the crowd into a boat waiting nearby, but authorities soon recaptured him. Tubman had to try again. She found out where he had been taken, and with the help of local citizens, both white and black, she stormed the house and managed to get Nalle out and onto a wagon heading west to Schenectady, New York. Money was later raised on Nalle's behalf to purchase his freedom.

CHAPTER FOUR

SERVING HER COUNTRY

Who else might need the services of "General" Tubman? After the first shots of the Civil War were fired over Fort Sumter, South Carolina, in April 1861, she would soon find out.

MOSES OF THE UNDERGROUND RISES ABOVE GROUND

Tubman served the Union Army during the Civil War. She nursed and cooked for both whites and blacks. Given her wide array of skills, she was at first vastly underutilized. But through the recommendations of prominent friends, eventually she was tapped to help put a spy network in place. She knew all about secret networks through her work with the Underground Railroad. By early 1863, she was given the job to scout out and map regions in South Carolina. She served as official commander of her men. She led her raiding parties in Confederate territory as the woman named Moses. And, as a spy, she provided strategic

This 1885 photo shows Tubman years after she served in the Union Army, a role John Brown may have predicted for her by calling her "General."

Tubman, holding a pan, is shown in this *New York Times* photograph with slaves she helped during the Civil War. It was taken circa 1887 outside Tubman's home in Auburn.

information about the Confederacy's position and its strengths and weaknesses.

Her scouting and spying came together in June 1863. She waited in darkness as Union gunboats moved through South Carolina. This was just like all those journeys she had made under the noses of slaveowners and slavecatchers to bring slaves to freedom. Now she guided the ships in their raid to seize torpedoes and empty warehouses. She also emptied plantations and 750 slaves boarded the federal gunboats with the help of 150 black soldiers. She was the first woman ever to lead an armed military raid. Moses had risen from the underground.

In July 1863, Union Army gunboats targeted the area in South Carolina where these slave cabins stand. Tubman helped save more than 700 slaves from this plantation.

But by spring 1864, Tubman requested leave to return home. Her health was failing and she worried about her elderly parents. She arrived in Auburn in the summer of 1864 with military transport all the way from South Carolina. She connected again with local friends there and in Boston. After several months at home, she was refreshed and ready to return to military duty. She joined Union forces in Virginia, again tending to the injured and sick. Soon after, however, the Confederacy surrendered and President Lincoln signed the Constitutional amendment to abolish slavery.

A LIFE IN PRINT

The first biography written about Harriet Tubman was published in 1869. Her friend Sarah Hopkins Bradford wrote it to help raise money for Tubman's support. They had met when Tubman returned home to Auburn in the summer of 1864. Without the pay for her war service, Tubman fell on hard times. To write the book, Bradford relied on her conversations with Tubman. She also gathered documents, including testimonies from participants in abolitionist and Underground Railroad activities. Some historians believe the volume was hastily written and published, as Bradford was preparing for a trip to Europe. A second version was published in 1886 as a result of Tubman's need for money to establish a shelter for aging African Americans. In this revision, now titled *Harriet Tubman: The Moses of Her People,* Bradford sought to elevate Tubman's speech to standard English. Historians have studied the two editions and debate whether either one reflects Tubman's truth.

NELSON DAVIS JOINS THE AUBURN HOUSEHOLD

Tubman met Nelson Davis in South Carolina during the war. Davis had escaped from slavery in North Carolina and found haven in New York State. He joined the New York Eighth Regiment and in 1864, his unit moved south. After the war, he made his way to Auburn and Tubman's house where she helped him recover from tuberculosis. Tubman

Although Tubman took a seat in Auburn, where this photo was taken, she stood up for her rights and successfully petitioned the US government for pay she deserved.

often took in other blacks who needed food, shelter, and medical help. He no doubt helped her deal with the news of her husband John Tubman's murder by a white man in Maryland in the fall of 1867. She focused on running her household and taking care of the people boarding with her.

Soon Davis and Tubman decided to marry. Unlike her first wedding, this one was recorded and took place in church in 1869. They were married until his death in 1888.

POSTWAR STRUGGLES

Tubman's military successes went largely unnoticed. Even on the journey home a New Jersey train conductor did not believe she was a returning soldier and he threw her into the baggage car. She knew tough struggles lay ahead. One of these struggles was trying to collect her back pay of $1,800. The US government refused to recognize her war service. It passed a law allowing war widows to claim a pension. Tubman applied for the pension and its usual amount of eight dollars a month. The US Congress debated her application. Both the House of Representatives and the US Senate wanted to give her more, but they had trouble agreeing on the amount. Finally, in 1899 President William McKinley signed her $20 monthly pension into law.

CHAPTER FIVE

HARRIET TUBMAN'S LEGACY

Tubman's health continued to plague her, yet she worked to support two schools for freed blacks in the South. She also continued to provide a home for her parents. At the same time, she devoted herself, too, to women's suffrage and frequently attended meetings. Tubman knew how to tell a story and keep her audiences riveted. She was sought after as a public speaker. But money was a persistent problem.

HER FINAL YEARS

With more and more people living under her roof while she tended to them, and with her commitments to schools and shelters, Tubman had to borrow money for food. Still, she must have taken comfort in her shelter for elderly blacks when its doors finally opened in Auburn in 1908. It was named appropriately the Harriet Tubman Home. Despite ill health, the generosity of those around her allowed Tubman to help blacks with nowhere else to go. Her efforts in the

Tubman's accomplishments loomed large, but the woman was aging, her health failing her. Still, she remained charismatic and sought after. There were still deeds to be done.

Tubman continued a life of service, even in her advanced years. She provided food and money to schools like this one, shown in 1911.

name of charity made her a role model in local eyes. Following her example, a home for black women opened in Boston bearing her name.

Even after the turn of the twentieth century, Tubman could be seen heading to the Auburn train station to attend a suffrage meeting elsewhere in New York State.

A LEGEND LIVES ON

Tubman died in Auburn on March 10, 1913, and was buried with military honors. She had already been made into a

In Harlem, New York, artist Alison Saar created this bronze statue of a determined Tubman on the move. Not seen from this view, the roots of inequality and tyranny are pulled from the ground as Tubman walks.

legend through newspaper and magazine articles and books written about her, as well as her own public appearances. At the core of her fame, of course, lay her role in risking her life to save other slaves. A statue was erected in Battle Creek, Michigan, where fellow former slave and abolitionist Sojourner Truth had lived. Another statue appeared in Boston. A year after her death, the city of Auburn unveiled a plaque on the Cayuga County Courthouse in her memory. Each year on Memorial Day weekend in May, people come to the African Methodist Episcopal Zion Church in Auburn to honor Tubman's life and achievements. The Harriet Tubman House, now owned by this church, has become a museum and education center. Another museum has been erected in Cambridge, Maryland, close to where Tubman was born. This museum celebrates March 10 as Harriet Tubman Day. A garden was planted along Cambridge's Highway and named the Harriet Tubman Memorial Garden.

To dedicate this garden in 2000, people made a pilgrimage from Maryland to New York to commemorate Tubman's many journeys. In Ontario, Canada, where she and her parents lived for a while, there is now a research facility at York University named the Harriet Tubman Resource Centre on the African Diaspora. In addition, the church Tubman attended in Canada placed a historical marker to remember her.

Many public schools bear Tubman's name. Year after year, schoolchildren learn about her by watching the play *Freedom*

MYTH OR FACT?

In many ways, Harriet Tubman appears larger than life. Her journeys have been made unrealistic, especially in books for children. Historians now believe that Tubman's journeys were more complicated and dangerous than originally thought. However, she did not travel throughout the South saving slaves. She returned only to Maryland and to plantations she knew. Many stories describe Tubman using quilts with codes sewed into them to guide slaves to the North. Tubman did not follow any secret quilt codes. Instead, the wily Tubman used her wits, the shape of the rivers, and the stars to show her the way. She also altered the tempos of spiritual songs such as "Go Down Moses" and "Bound for the Promised Land," using the songs to deliver messages to passengers on the Underground Railroad. Making the sound of an owl was another one of her signals. Another myth is that she started the Underground Railroad. While she didn't start it, Tubman helped expand the already existing network and became its most famous conductor. Tubman herself, however, was more proud of her work with the Union Army.

Train or other dramatic productions. But everyone will learn about her in 2020 when Harriet Tubman's face appears on the US $20 bill, replacing that of Andrew Jackson.

IMMORTAL THROUGH ART

In the 1930s, African American artist Jacob Lawrence told the story of Harriet Tubman through a series of thirty-one paintings. Inspired by the tales he heard from elders in New York City's Harlem community, he wanted to portray "Moses" as art. He believed Tubman's story was one of America's great sagas. To tell her story, he combined

Artist Jacob Lawrence, shown here in his studio in 1989, used his particular style of visual storytelling to honor Harriet Tubman and her life.

pictures and text. Social injustice was a frequent subject of his artwork.

MOSES OF HER PEOPLE

Although perhaps a mythical figure to many, Harriet Tubman was a real-life Moses for hundreds of former slaves. Thousands of African Americans today can trace their families' freedom to Tubman. There are also those who are descended from soldiers she helped while serving in the Union Army and those she housed at the Auburn shelter. Tubman's fierce determination helped her beat the odds against her, whether she was facing a bounty placed on her head by slave owners, the threat of Confederate capture, or the financial challenges involved in her later efforts to provide for others and stand up for what was right. Tubman is proof that one woman can make a tremendous difference and change the course of history.

GLOSSARY

abolitionist A person who supported the end of slavery.

African diaspora Communities of people descended from those taken from their African homelands as slaves.

bounty Money given as a reward.

commemorate To honor the memory of someone, usually with some kind of ceremony and marker.

emancipation To free from slavery or bondage.

fugitive Someone who runs away from a bad situation.

Mennonite Member of a specific Protestant sect, known for being against war.

Methodist Member of a large Christian denomination believing in strong social morals.

militia People called into duty to serve in the military.

pension An allowance paid at regular intervals.

pilgrimage A long journey to a specific place, sometimes made for religious reasons.

Quaker The name for a member of the Society of Friends, a Christian group with a long tradition of actively working for peace and opposing war.

saga A tale of heroic achievements and events.

stamina A degree of physical strength that allows an individual the power to endure.

suffrage The right to vote in a political election.

testimonies Statements made by witnesses of an event or about a person.

treason An act to overthrow the government.

underutilize Failure to use an individual's skills and talents to their best advantage.

West Indies A group of islands situated between North and South America that border the Caribbean Sea.

FOR FURTHER READING

Adler, David. *Harriet Tubman and the Underground Railroad*. New York, NY: Holiday House, 2012.

Baumann, Susan K. *Harriet Tubman: Conductor of the Underground Railroad* (Junior Graphic African American History). New York, NY: PowerKids Press, 2013.

Cummings, Judy Dodge and Tom Casteel (illus.). *The Underground Railroad: Navigate the Journey from Slavery to Freedom* (Build It Yourself). White River Junction, VT: Nomad Press, 2017.

Doak, Robin S. *Harriet Tubman* (True Bookbiographies). New York, NY: Scholastic, 2015.

Hale, Nathan. *The Underground Abductor: An Abolitionist Tale about Harriet Tubman* (Nathan Hale's Hazardous Tales). New York, NY: Harry N. Abrams, 2015.

McDonnell, Julia. *Harriet Tubman in Her Own Words* (Eyewitness to History). New York, NY: Gareth Stevens, 2016.

McDonough, Yona Zeldis, Lauren Mortimer (illus.), and James Bennett (illus.). *What Was the Underground Railroad?* New York, NY: Grosset & Dunlap/Penguin, 2013.

Norwich, Grace. *I Am Harriet Tubman*. New York, NY: Scholastic, 2013.

WEBSITES

Because of the changing nature of internet links, Rosen Publishing has developed an online list of websites related to the subject of this book. This site is updated regularly. Please use this link to access this list:

http://www.rosenlinks.com/WWCH/tubman

INDEX